Out *of* Eden

Out *of* Eden

7 Ways God Restores Blocked Communication

Healing Relationships:
From Isolation to Connection

Paul A. Soukup, S.J.

Art by Jenny Hodgson McGee

Pauline
BOOKS & MEDIA
Boston

Library of Congress Cataloging-in-Publication Data

Soukup, Paul A.

  Out of Eden : 7 ways God restores blocked communication / Paul A.
Soukup.

      p. cm.

  ISBN 0-8198-6484-6 (pbk.)

  1. Interpersonal communication—Religious aspects—Christianity.
2. Spiritual life—Christianity. I. Title.

  BV4597.53.C64S68 2006

  248—dc22

                                        2006009282

The Scripture quotations contained herein are from the *New Revised
Standard Version Bible: Catholic Edition*, copyright © 1989, 1993, Division of
Christian Education of the National Council of the Churches of Christ in
the United States of America. Used by permission. All rights reserved.

Cover design by Rosana Usselmann

Photo credit: ©image100 Ltd

"P" and PAULINE are registered trademarks of the Daughters of St. Paul.

Published by Pauline Books & Media, 50 Saint Paul's Avenue, Boston, MA
02130-3491. www.pauline.org.

Printed in the U.S.A.

Pauline Books & Media is the publishing house of the Daughters of St. Paul,
an international congregation of women religious serving the Church with
the communications media.

1 2 3 4 5 6 7 8 9   11 10 09 08 07 06

*I'd like to thank the people of Saint Joseph of Cupertino parish,
who accompanied me through Lent; the Santa Clara University
students enrolled in my communication and theology class,
who taught me that we need to share stories like these;
and Mary Novak and Bob Hodgson, who suggested ways
to improve this work.*

Contents

Introduction

GOD WANTS TO COMMUNICATE WITH US.

Theologians tell us about the self-communication of God: the material self-communication of God in creation and the verbal self-communication of God in revelation. But what it all really means is that God reaches out to us, that he loves us, and that God wants to evoke our love. As we know from talking with one another, true communication expects a response. And so, when God communicates with us, God invites us to communicate.

Our history—both the history of the human race and our personal history—becomes the history of that communication…and, sadly, of our resistance to God's self-communication. Not surprisingly, a failure in communication with God goes hand in hand with the breakdown in communication among humans.

God's salvation not only restores the broken communication with God but also among ourselves.

We are, after all, the same persons as we communicate with God and with one another. This exactly parallels what we read in the First Letter of John, "We love, because God first loved us. If any one says, 'I love God,' and hates his brother, he is a liar; for he who does not love his brother whom he has seen, cannot love God whom he has not seen" (1 Jn 4: 19–20). Restoring communication with God moves us toward healing the rifts in interpersonal communication. And, conversely, restoring communication with each other moves us toward restoring communication with God. God's salvation not only restores the broken communication with God but also among ourselves. The theme of God communicating to us has, then, very real day-to-day human consequences.

These reflections on God's self-communication and our response began during Lent, led by the Scriptures of that time of reflection, Scriptures used particularly for the preparation of those seeking baptism. Though it is an exceptional time to examine God's communication and our responses, it is not the only time. God wants to communicate with us all the time, and these reflections can be used in any liturgical season or at any time in our lives. Whenever you choose to use them, the idea is to read and hear the Scriptures through the lens of communication.

As we begin, then, let us pray, adapting Saint Augustine's words, "Dear Lord, teach us to know ourselves, to know how we communicate; teach us to know you, to know how you communicate. Teach us to love ourselves; teach us to love you."

CHAPTER ONE

Why Is Communication So Hard?

The Basic Temptation: Suspicion Over Trust

GENESIS 3:1–8

Now the serpent was more crafty than any other wild animal that the LORD God had made. He said to the woman, "Did God say, 'You shall not eat from any tree in the garden'?" The woman said to the serpent, "We may eat of the fruit of the trees in the garden; but God said, 'You shall not eat of the fruit of the tree that is in the midst of the garden, nor shall you touch it, or you shall die.'" But the serpent said to the woman, "You will not die; for God knows that when you eat of it your eyes will be opened, and you will be like God, knowing good and evil." So when the woman saw that the tree was good for food, and that it was a delight to the eyes, and that the tree was to be desired to make one wise, she took of its fruit and ate; and she also gave some to her husband, who was with her, and he ate. Then the eyes of both were opened, and they knew that they were naked; and they sewed fig leaves together and made loincloths for themselves.

They heard the sound of the LORD God walking in the garden at the time of the evening breeze, and the man and his wife hid themselves from the presence of the LORD God among the trees of the garden.

MATTHEW 4:1–4

Then Jesus was led up by the Spirit into the wilderness to be tempted by the devil. He fasted forty days and forty nights, and afterward he was famished. The tempter came and said to him, "If you are the Son of God, command these stones to become loaves of bread." But he answered, "It is written, 'One does not live by bread alone, but by every word that comes from the mouth of God.'"

WE BEGIN, AS SCRIPTURAL REFLECTIONS often do, in the garden. God has created us; the world is new; there's a freshness about. God, we are told, saw that it was good. Genesis goes on to tell us that God was in the habit of walking in the garden in the cool of the evening. Eve and Adam would walk with God and, we can suppose, converse with God, as friends might. There's a wonderful image of intimacy in those conversations. God, Eve, Adam at peace with one another, enjoying this simple moment. In

The idea of communication beckons us, the ease of it, the idealness of it.

those walks, we have an image of communication: simple, direct, open, deepening a friendship, leading to a loving exchange. Communication occurs almost without effort for God, Adam, and Eve.

We may think of those moments with a kind of nostalgia. How good things were then! And maybe we find similar moments in our lives. How we spoke to one another at first love, how parents and children shared the simple things that brought joy to all, how we worked easily with colleagues, trading ideas. The idea of such communication beckons us, the ease of it, the *idealness* of it.

Its being an *ideal* suggests that such communication no longer exists. What happened?

The Genesis account tells us. One day Eve and Adam began to listen to another voice in the garden, a voice that was not God's voice (the voice of the tempter, we later learn). The message didn't matter; only the question in the voice. "Did God really say that?" the tempter asks, all the while implying, "Can you really trust God?" That other voice suggests that God's communication has a purpose other than the simple sharing, friends with friends, lovers calling to one another. The other voice whispers that God's communication is set to enslave you, forbidding you to eat of this tree, forbidding you that knowledge. Better to be suspicious than to be duped.

And so they listened to that other voice. God came to walk again in the garden. And Adam and Eve hid themselves. They cut off the communication. Or, rather, the communication had been cut off since that other voice raised a suspicion in their minds: What is God really up to?

That same suspicion enters into all our human communication, doesn't it? We're never quite sure about any communication. First love gives way to routine or (worse yet) jealousy. The "other voice" is the voice of Iago muttering in Othello's ear: *She'll only hurt you. He'll betray you.* Children find their parents a bit boring, especially compared with their friends or with the television or with music. Parents wonder about their children: You just can't talk to teens, they think. Our co-workers are out to advance themselves, to follow some agenda we don't quite recognize. The "other voice" tells us to beware. And we do. We erect a barrier to communication.

We listen to a lot of other voices: voices that tell us to doubt ourselves, to find ourselves in what we possess, to judge our value by how we look, to question the motives of others, to look out for ourselves. There are more dangerous voices, too: voices telling us not to forget past hurts, voices whispering against forgiveness, voices seeking revenge. Those voices block us in, block out the possibility of communication.

In his commentary on this in Romans 5, Saint Paul says that death enters at this moment. It certainly marks the death of communication, what some have called the death of language. What should be so transparent, so easy, becomes clouded with suspicion. We make what is a natural part of us, what should connect us to each other, into a tool, an instrument to separate from us that we wield in order to protect ourselves. We isolate ourselves and speak a careful language, one that is hemmed in, one filled with measured and limited phrases. We'd rather die than let someone take advantage of us.

And always at the heart of it the other voice asks, "Can you trust?"

And so we enter into a pattern of blocked communication. Perhaps we recognize the possibility of communication as we remember the ideal. We sense ourselves drawn to God's self-communication just as we sense ourselves desiring a genuine communication with each other. But it is blocked.

Our first look at God's self-communication and our turning away ends, as every meditation should, with God's response. Where there is blocked communication, God acts to restore it.

We come then, with Jesus, led into the desert by the Holy Spirit. Here we see Jesus open to God, letting God show the way. Jesus spends those forty days alone with God, perhaps reliving the walks with God in the garden, but now the garden is no more, dried up into a desert by the lack of communication. The tempter comes again, as it has in every generation and to every one of us who longs for communication. The words differ but the message stays the same: "If you are the son, beloved of God, why are you hungry?" Again, mistrust is what the tempter implies: "Don't trust God to feed you. Better do it yourself." But Jesus, God's own Word made flesh, reminds us of the priorities in our living: "We don't live by bread alone, but by every word that comes from the mouth of God." Listen to one voice. Listen to the voice of God.

Where there is blocked communication, God acts to restore it.

Here is how God reacts to our suspicion. Here is how God reacts to our blocked communication: he leads us to discover the voice to

which we should listen. It's not the voice of power; it's not the voice challenging God; it's not the voice that would possess the world and its treasures. It's not the voice of suspicion. But it is the word of God.

We should remember that this word of God is not what we think of as a "word." Too many years of reading have shrunk the word to a "word"—a few letters surrounded by spaces. For Jesus, the "word" was not that brief thing. As a member of a culture less familiar with writing, for Jesus the "word" is really the act of speaking, the discourse or—better yet—the conversation. The "word" becomes a way of living, and that way of living becomes a relationship.

The antidote to the death of communication and language is the conversation. And every conversation requires cooperation, working together, and trust.

The antidote to the death of communication and language is conversation. And every conversation requires cooperation, working together, and trust

Instead of hearing the tempter's doubt—Can you trust God?—we are invited into a conversation, a relationship. The trust will come as the conversation continues.

That same saving offer occurs in our day-to-day lives as well. Conversation is a real possibility, if we can set aside our focus on ourselves and our fears. Think of the chances: once again, loving conversations, conversations about love, gifts of talk to children, renewed discovery of parents, talks with colleagues, dialogues among governments, opportunities for peace.

God acts to overcome blocked communication by offering us a Word.

Deepening Our Communication

The antidote to the death of communication and language is the conversation. And every conversation requires cooperation, working together, and trust. Instead of hearing the tempter's doubt—Can you trust God?—we are invited into a conversation, a relationship. The trust will come as the conversation continues. That same saving offer occurs in our day-to-day lives as well. Conversation is a real possibility, if we can set aside our focus on ourselves and our fears. Think of the chances: once again, loving conversations, conversations about love, gifts of talk to children, renewed discovery of parents, talks with colleagues, dialogues among governments, opportunities for peace. (page 12)

1. Think about a conversation you'd like to have with someone. Really think about it—the person, the topic, the goal. Write down what is stopping you from having this conversation, thoughts such as: *"He may not forgive me; she always avoids me; they will make a scene; I will be rejected."* Ask yourself: What is the deepest fear and the deepest desire underlying the reasons you listed for the above question that keep you from communication?

2. Trust builds upon ordinary things. We usually
    aim too high, want too much, want it too fast.
    Start with something simple. Conversations are
    ongoing. How could you open up one of these
    conversations? What could happen if you did?

3. What suspicions do you have that prevent or
    distort communication? If these suspicions
    had voices, what would they be saying to you?
    What areas of your life are suffering because
    you are listening to these suspicions?

4. In the Scripture reading at the beginning of
    this chapter, the devil's voice injects suspicion,
    jealousy, and fear into the communication
    between God and his creatures. In the reading
    from the Gospel of Matthew, we learn that
    "God leads us to discover the voice to which
    we should listen." Spend some time in quiet
    prayer, listening for this voice within yourself.
    Sink deeply within yourself to that place
    where trust still exists between you and God,
    you and others. What is this place like?

Prayer

Dear Lord,
we need to talk.
Part of talking is listening,
but all too often we want you to listen to us talk.
Help us to change that.
Speak to us now.
Teach us why we would rather listen
to voices other than yours.
Why do we want to listen to those who doubt us
or doubt your love?
Show us what's so attractive in those voices.
Show us what moves our hearts away from you.
Show us what blocks our communication
—with you, with each other—
and then teach us again how to listen, how to talk.
Through Jesus, teach us your word.
Let us listen again to your voice, and as we hear
you, may we hear each other, too,
but with trusting ears.

CHAPTER TWO

What Keeps Us from Listening to Each Other?

Personal Communication

MATTHEW 17:1–9

Six days later, Jesus took with him Peter and James and his brother John and led them up a high mountain, by themselves. And he was transfigured before them, and his face shone like the sun, and his clothes became dazzling white. Suddenly there appeared to them Moses and Elijah, talking with him. Then Peter said to Jesus, "Lord, it is good for us to be here; if you wish, I will make three dwellings here, one for you, one for Moses, and one for Elijah." While he was still speaking, suddenly a bright cloud overshadowed them, and from the cloud a voice said, "This is my Son, the Beloved; with him I am well pleased; listen to him!" When the disciples heard this, they fell to the ground and were overcome by fear. But Jesus came and touched them, saying, "Get up and do not be afraid." And when they looked up, they saw no one except Jesus himself alone.

As they were coming down the mountain, Jesus ordered them, "Tell no one about the vision until after the Son of Man has been raised from the dead."

WE MIGHT EXPECT THAT JESUS—the Word of God— would have an easy time with communication. But that's not always the case, as we see and hear in Matthew 17, where Jesus takes Peter, James, and John to a high mountain where, Matthew matter-of-factly narrates, Jesus is transfigured before them. One thing is consistent: here as elsewhere God takes the initiative in restoring blocked communication. Jesus invites them.

In the midst of this stunning portrayal, we can easily overlook what happens to the communication. Jesus is transfigured. Clothes become dazzlingly white; his face glows. Moses and Elijah appear.

And the communication blockage shows up too. As he so often does in the Gospels, Peter represents all of us. Here, his communication behavior seems so natural...and, on reflection, so wrong. He begins describing, planning, speaking almost as if he doesn't know what he's saying. And, finally, God has to interrupt him to get a word in edgewise. "This is my Son, the Beloved. Listen to him."

Listen. Ah, now we begin to see the blocked communication. It's the same blockage that works among us: in families, at work, in the Church. Let's examine it more closely, to understand why Peter's natural mode (our own natural mode) works against communication. Why doesn't Peter communicate?

First, the narrative is pretty clear: he's too busy talking. Peter's impulse is to talk. He doesn't mean ill; he just wants to fill the time, fill the silences, fill the excitement-caused tension and smooth it out. "Lord, it's good for us to be here." Yes, it is, but Peter's commentary isn't really necessary and competes with what God would tell him. And as Peter talks, he doesn't know what he's saying, so there is no conversation. It's a one-way exercise, a monologue. How often we talk the same way: not much to say, but better than silence, we think. If we wonder about the blockages to our own communication, we might reflect for a moment on how we talk. What do we say? When do we say it? What's going on around us? How does our talking relate to the others with us?

How often do we, like Peter, not allow what's happening around us really to register in our minds because we're busy thinking about the next step or wondering what we'll say next...

Second, Peter doesn't communicate because he's too busy planning, too busy thinking one step ahead. "Let us build three dwellings here, one for you, one for Moses, one for Elijah." This doesn't mean that planning ahead is bad, just that our planning can block our listening. How often do we, like Peter, not allow what's happening around us really to register in our minds because we're busy thinking about the next step or wondering what we'll say next, what we'll do for dinner, or about tomorrow's meeting. We may be physically present to our companions, but not mentally, not spiritually. We may call it multitasking, and we may even pride ourselves on it. But we should ask what those habits do to our ability to communicate. The plan takes precedence over the people. It's not only a personal failing, but an institutional one as well. We get quite good at strategic plans; we can keep the goals and what we see as the good of the institution in mind, but somehow the people can feel left out, just things or pawns to be factored into the strategy.

Third, we literally see a failure of communication here on the mountaintop. Peter doesn't communicate because he, and the other disciples, let the image seduce them: Jesus transfigured, clothes brighter than light. It's worth seeing. Again, we shouldn't conclude that seeing or images are bad. But we should be realistic and ask ourselves how we react to images. The hypnotic look can block our listening—as God reminds the disciples. It's not unlike how we sometimes regard television. The wonder of it dazzles us, the quality of the images fascinates us, the sheer movement of it captivates us...and blocks our communication. How often have we let the television monopolize our attention to the detriment of those with us? The problem is not the image nor the tool, but what we do with them. Remember God's response to Peter and the others who had focused on the transfigured image: Listen to him.

Finally, we learn a deeper reason for the failure to communicate, for the blockage that characterizes how we come before God and before one another. Peter, James, and John were afraid, Matthew tells us.

*When we fall in love...
we open up the pathways
of communication
and, sometimes
without effort,
we change.*

They fell to the ground and hid their faces. (Just like Eve and Adam in the garden, after they had listened to that other voice. They, too, knew fear and hid their faces from God.) Our fears do indeed block our communication. We may well be perfectly able to listen to one another and to speak out from our hearts, but we are afraid. "What will she say? What will he tell me? Do I really want to hear it?" I need to protect myself...and my fears begin to take on a life of their own. Those fears keep me from others and from God. We construct a whole taxonomy of fear, reasons to block out most communication, most words of address, except those around which we feel safe (the ones we can control).

Perhaps this explains why love is such a surprise to us. We learn that we can trust another and that communication can touch our hearts and open our minds. This is why conversion is led by love: when we fall in love—whether with God, with another, with God's people, with the poor, with anyone—we open up the pathways of communication and, sometimes without effort, we change.

Here is a lesson of the transfigured Jesus. The opening of communication leads to love and that love leads to accompanying Jesus, overcoming fear. "Don't be afraid," he tells the disciples. And then, "Don't tell the others until the Son of Man has been raised from the dead." Listening to Jesus will give rise to a deeper love that will take them through his death to his rising. In retrospect, even though they did not handle the passion of Jesus well, the apostles learned to listen to him and to take courage, a courage that characterizes their lives from the rising of Jesus to their own deaths. Love alone leads them. And that love lets them listen.

Love counters the blocked communication. Perhaps it is slow in coming, perhaps it is only learned over time, but love quiets us. When we listen, really listen to another, we need not talk or plan or watch or fear.

This unblocking of communication happens here on the personal level. Which of my actions block communication? Which of God's actions counter that?

God takes the initiative to unblock communication. Here we contemplate God's action not in a restoration of health as we find in the healing miracles of Jesus, but in a restoration of hearing. We see God's action in the word, "Listen to him." God was not put off by Peter's talking, by his planning, by his focus on image, or even by his fear. It was enough to say, "Listen to him." It was enough to touch them and raise them up from their fear. Listening led to love, and love, to listening.

Deepening Our Communication

Peter doesn't communicate because he's too busy planning, too busy thinking one step ahead. "Let us build three dwellings here, one for you, one for Moses, one for Elijah." This doesn't mean that planning ahead is bad, just that our planning can block our listening. How often do we, like Peter, not allow what's happening around us really to register in our minds because we're busy thinking about the next step or wondering what we'll say next, what we'll do for dinner, or about tomorrow's meeting. We may be physically present to our companions, but not mentally, not spiritually. We may call it multitasking, and we may even pride ourselves on it. But we should ask what these habits do to our ability to communicate. The plan takes precedence over the people. (page 20)

1. How comfortable are you with silence? Picture a recent incident that involved a communication problem. What part did you play in it? Did your reactions have some of the characteristics of Peter at the Transfiguration? Knowing ourselves, even laughing at ourselves a bit, is the first step toward life-giving communication.

2. Look for examples of your communication and noncommunication behaviors. Observe your thoughts, feelings, and impulses when another person is speaking with you. Make a note of these. Do they differ according to the person who is speaking? Do you have communication characteristics that are consistent no matter who is speaking? What are they? Try to observe your pattern of communication with others when you are bored by the speaker or the topic of conversation. When you feel threatened. When there is a television in the room. When you are reading the paper or working. When the other is sharing difficult personal information. When you are being confronted for something you have done. Make your own personal list of communication blocks.

3. Fear often characterizes unhealthy communication. When two people are in love, the love they feel toward one another helps them overcome fear and remove blocks in communication. Can you remember experiencing love from a parent or grandparent, fiancé or friend?

How would you describe your communication with this person?

4. In the Scripture passage on the Transfiguration, God restores Peter's hearing, by telling him, "Listen." Spend some time in silent, prayerful listening. What do you hear? Probably chattering, planning, and rehearsing of past or future events. These patterns of communication also block our communion with God. Fear lies at the bottom of all this "wordiness." God invites us to trust in his love for us. Gently let go of everything you are holding on to, those things which precipitate the endless chatter and planning that interrupt our conversation with God: events, worries, ambitions, ideals, dreams, anger, the past, the future. Take several deep breaths and relax into the silence, listening.

Prayer

O Lord,
how often do we resemble Peter?
    Talking...yes, we love to talk,
    but you made us that way.
    Planning ahead...yes, how else will we live?
    Seduced by images...yes, that too,
    and you made sight a precious gift.
    Afraid...yes, even when we don't want
        to admit it.
Help us to understand ourselves.
We want to listen to you, to one another,
but we don't.
Help us to see ourselves as you see us.
Let us feel Jesus' gentle touch to rouse us.
Let us hear him reassure us that we need not
    be afraid,
especially with your communication.
Yes, let us listen to him.

CHAPTER THREE

How Do We Build Trust?

Interpersonal Communication

JOHN 4:1–42

Now when Jesus learned that the Pharisees had heard, "Jesus is making and baptizing more disciples than John"—although it was not Jesus himself but his disciples who baptized—he left Judea and started back to Galilee. But he had to go through Samaria. So he came to a Samaritan city called Sychar, near the plot of ground that Jacob gave to his son Joseph.

Jacob's well was there, and Jesus, tired out by his journey, was sitting by the well. It was about noon.

A Samaritan woman came to draw water, and Jesus said to her, "Give me a drink." (His disciples had gone to the city to buy food.) The Samaritan woman said to him, "How is it that you, a Jew, ask a drink of me, a woman of Samaria?" (Jews do not share things in common with Samaritans.) Jesus answered her, "If you knew the gift of God, and who it is that is saying to you, 'Give me a drink,' you would have asked him, and he would have given you living water." The woman said to him, "Sir, you have no bucket, and the well is deep; where do you get that living water? Are you greater than our ancestor Jacob, who gave us the well, and with his sons and his flocks drank from it?"

Jesus said to her, "Everyone who drinks of this water will be thirsty again, but those who drink of the water that I will give them will never be thirsty. The water that I will give will become in them a spring of water gushing up to eternal life." The woman said to him, "Sir, give me this water, so that I may never be thirsty or have to keep coming here to draw water."

Jesus said to her, "Go, call your husband, and come back." The woman answered him, "I have no husband." Jesus said to her, "You are right in saying, 'I have no husband'; for you have had five husbands, and the one you have now is not your husband.

"What you have said is true!" The woman said to him, "Sir, I see that you are a prophet. Our ancestors worshiped on this mountain, but you say that the place where people must worship is in Jerusalem." Jesus said to her, "Woman, believe me, the hour is coming when you will worship the Father neither on this mountain nor in Jerusalem. You worship what you do not know; we worship what we know, for salvation is from the Jews. But the hour is coming, and is now here, when the true worshipers will worship the Father in spirit and truth, for the Father seeks such as these to worship him. God is spirit, and those who worship him must worship in spirit and truth." The woman said to him, "I know that Messiah is coming" (who is called Christ). "When he comes, he will proclaim all things to us." Jesus said to her, "I am he, the one who is speaking to you."

Just then his disciples came. They were astonished that he was speaking with a woman, but no one said, "What do you want?" or, "Why are you speaking with her?" Then the woman left her water jar and went back to the city. She said to the people, "Come and see a man who told me everything that I have ever done! He cannot be the Messiah, can he?" They left the city and were on their way to him.

Meanwhile the disciples were urging him, "Rabbi, eat something." But he said to them, "I have food to eat that you do not know about." So the disciples said to one another, "Surely no one has brought him something to eat?" Jesus said to them, "My food is to do the will of him who sent me and to complete his work. Do you not say, 'Four months more, then comes the harvest'? But I tell you, look around you, and see how the fields are ripe for harvesting. The reaper is already receiving wages and is gathering fruit for eternal life, so that sower and reaper may rejoice together. For here the saying holds true, 'One sows and another reaps.' I sent you to reap that for which you did not labor. Others have labored, and you have entered into their labor."

Many Samaritans from that city believed in him because of the woman's testimony, "He told me everything I have ever done." So when the Samaritans came to him, they asked him to stay with them; and he stayed there two days. And many more believed because of his word. They said to the woman, "It is no longer because of what you said that we believe, for we have heard for ourselves, and we know that this is truly the Savior of the world."

BY NOW WE SHOULD RECOGNIZE the pattern. God wants to communicate with us. But that communication is blocked as we raise barriers, not only against him, but against one another as well. So, God takes the initiative to reestablish communication.

In this third moment, we see more clearly the causes and consequences of our communication blockages, and we can watch Jesus taking the initiative to overcome those blockages. It's a simple setting in many ways: Jesus and the disciples are traveling from Jerusalem back to Galilee, walking a familiar road, through Samaria. But no matter how familiar the road, it's a strange journey, as John tells us, since Jews don't have anything to do with Samaritans. Imagine not speaking with the neighbors. Imagine having to walk with suspicion, hand-on-your-wallet kind of walking. Well, perhaps it's not so difficult to imagine, for we too have neighbors we won't speak with, neighbors we distrust. Perhaps they are from the wrong country; perhaps they are the wrong race; perhaps they speak the wrong language or don't speak ours well at all; perhaps they worship at the wrong church or at no church at all; perhaps they earn less than we (or more!); perhaps they are not as smart; perhaps they hold opinions we don't like. They're different. We just don't have anything to do with them.

Here, of course, everything we've learned about stereotypes comes into play. But it doesn't seem to matter that we understand this on a theoretical level...we still don't have much to do with people who are different from ourselves.

And so it was with the Jews and the Samaritans. The surprising thing about Jesus and the Samaritans is that he spoke of them at all. But he speaks of them and to them. Remember in Luke's Gospel, Jesus makes a Samaritan the neighbor in a parable to explain the meaning of the commandment, "Love your neighbor as yourself."

Back to the Gospel. Jesus and the disciples, tired from their journey, stop to rest by the well. The disciples leave to buy food (no doubt moving in a group to defend themselves, wary of the Samaritan villagers). Jesus has the self-confidence to remain alone by the well. A woman from the village comes to the well. And Jesus asks her for a drink of water. It's an ordinary request, much like asking a stranger, "Where's the bus stop?" or "How do I get downtown from here?" or "What time is it?" But John reminds us that it's not so ordinary. "Jews don't talk to Samaritans," he tells us. Even the woman is surprised. So this ordinary question on one level represents something much greater: Jesus' willingness to cross the boundaries of our blocked communication. If there is a blockage, he not only takes the initiative, but he goes through the blockage. And once he's started, the woman responds. Here is the beginning of dialogue.

The Swiss Biblical scholar Marc Chappuis (author of *Jesus et la Samaritaine*) says that this encounter represents seven different kinds of communication, ranging from this ordinary one to the revelation of God's saving power in the Messiah. Following his lead, let's think about what happens when God acts to break though the walls we build to block communication.

We've already seen the ordinary. Jesus asks for a drink of water, initiating a dialogue. The remarkable thing here is that Jesus' risk of communicating with a stranger is not all that different from what we are willing to do. It demands a certain trust, but only in the language we use and in the presumption that the person we're speaking with will respond honestly. "Where's the bus stop?" "A block up and turn at the corner." "What time is it?" "Two-thirty." It may not seem much, but it forms the first step in establishing a trust in our ability to communicate, and it demonstrates the resiliency of language. Even when we block communication and would seek the death of language, language refuses to die. In some ways, we have to begin with the most ordinary things and then discover that they can form the basis for something more.

This is where Jesus' communication with the woman shows the way. And here she, too, deserves some

We have to begin with the most ordinary things [in conversation] and then discover that they can form the basis for something more.

credit. Instead of simply giving Jesus the water, she asks him why he would speak with her, why he would cross that boundary erected between their two peoples. Jesus then takes another risk and moves their conversation from the ordinary, safe, matter-of-fact level to an interpersonal level. He begins to speak with the woman about who he is and who she is. His conversation now begins a process of self-disclosure.

Self-disclosure holds a central place in all true communication. Each of us must reveal what is within ourselves, the richness that makes us who we are and that distinguishes us from others. Such a disclosure can only appear as a gift—it's not something that another can demand, much less take from us. But without it, real communication can never appear.

Self-disclosure comes gradually, since it carries a certain risk with it. We disclose as we are ready, as we grow in trust of one another. Too much disclosure puts us off; too little leaves us at the level of the ordinary. With friends and family, we tell how we feel, what we think, what we ponder, what we love, what we fear...all of those things that make us who we are. And we hear the same from them. Researchers tell us that self-disclosure functions at its best reciprocally. Jesus and the Samaritan woman model that for us: each of them speaks to the heart of the other, not judgmentally and not in any attempt to exert power over the other. They give freely and speak of their thirst, their weariness, their desires, their religious longings. Just as we have to learn all other things, we can learn self-disclosure and its pacing here.

The lessons of self-disclosure affect not just our most intimate communication (though they are essential there), they also work in every kind of communication, though we may disclose different things at work, in our recreations, with friends, with family members. Self-disclosure rests on trust, on our willingness to listen to the voice of another and not to let ourselves become distracted by listening to those other voices that lead to the walls separating Samaritans and Jews, men and women, friends and foes.

Jesus' conversation with the woman of Samaria demonstrates yet another way in which God works to break down the blockages of communication among us. It's not enough to restore communication or even to share self-disclosure. Jesus easily (and much more easily than we ever seem capable of doing) says something about the woman, something that she knew but would not have volunteered. He continues, too, telling her things that she does not know or does not recognize about herself. The communication moves to helping her to see herself, not in a threatening way, but in a way that allows her to ask those things that really matter to her. In a way, Jesus sets her free to give voice to what matters most to her.

In this light, communication appears as a sacred trust, motivated not by the power of one partner to dominate the other, not by any desire to monopolize the conversation, but by the desire to let conversational partners speak what most concerns them. In this communication, we open the door for another by humbling ourselves. It is a communication based in love, with a regard for another that seeks the other's benefit. It very much models the description of Jesus in the hymn in Paul's Letter to the Philippians—he humbled himself to take on human form, communicating with us from within human experience, not asking us to change, but accepting our human condition so as to communicate better with us. (The Pontifical Council on Social Communication calls this, "the giving of the self in love," in *Communio et Progressio,* no. 8.) This kind of communication requires a change in attitude on our part, so that we begin seeking the good of the other.

Such truly personal communication also demands that we learn to put the best possible interpretation on another's communication. In this, we can learn from Saint Ignatius Loyola's *Spiritual Exercises.* Saint Ignatius calls

In this light, communication appears as a sacred trust.... It is a communication based in love, with a regard for another that seeks the other's benefit.

them exercises "because, as walking, going, and running are bodily exercises, in like manner all methods of preparing and disposing the soul...to seek and find the divine will...are called spiritual exercises." They are a series of meditations and reflections on the Scriptures undertaken with a spiritual director over the course of a month in which the retreatant seeks to find God's will and to set aside self-will. In the Presupposition to the Spiritual Exercises, Saint Ignatius tells the retreatant and the spiritual director that where there is uncertainty, we give the benefit of the doubt to one another, asking for explanation where we don't understand or cannot find a positive meaning. In other words, we set aside the built-in suspicion of our communication, the suspicion introduced by the tempter's voice.

The conversation between the Samaritan woman and Jesus leads from the truly personal to deeper questions. She builds on the trust they now have to ask Jesus about her ultimate concerns. "I see you are a prophet, sir." And then she can ask all those other questions. Why do we regard God as we do? Why do peoples differ in their understanding of God? How do we worship God? How do we know God? What would God have us do? For her, these are not casual questions, but questions that define the very basis of living. They are also our questions, rooted in the quiet places in our hearts, questions that touch on our very identity as humans. We need to talk about them, but so often we hesitate.

These questions demand trust of one another, and we really cannot pose them until we know one another through the processes of conversation and self-disclosure and loving acceptance. But they are possible. There's another thing here that we should note now: the process of conversation matters as much to the woman as the answers that Jesus gives her. The disciples don't quite seem to understand that—they marveled at it, but at least they didn't interrupt. The process also matters to Jesus: it fulfilled his need for food. As the will of his Father, this work to unblock communication satisfied his thirst and his hunger. All too often it's tempting to find *our* satisfaction in God's work to unblock communication and to forget God's satisfaction. The process should move us to take on the perspective of the other—and that includes God's perspective.

How do we worship God? How do we know God? What would God have us do? These questions touch on our very identity as humans.

The end of the conversation with Jesus leads the woman into other conversations. She goes back to the village, telling others about Jesus and about her conversation. She now begins to act as Jesus acts, restoring communication with those around her. She discloses (voluntarily and without fear) what the others perhaps already knew and held against her ("he told me everything I have ever done"). But now she does not seek herself or her plan; instead she brings people to Jesus. Like Jesus, she aims for their good.

The removal of the blockage of communication for the woman of Samaria has consequences for the whole village of Samaria...and for all Samaritans. Communication restored affects not just the two who are communicating, but all humans.

Here Jesus' saving action unfolds in a simple way. He breaks down a wall of separation, one request at a time, one word after another, inviting us into conversation, inviting us to take first a small risk to reveal something of ourselves while he reveals himself. From there he leads us deeper, ever deeper into the mystery of God, into the self-communication of God that creates us and speaks to us. Seated by the well, Jesus recreates the garden where we and God once spoke easily—in a conversation, listening and talking.

Deepening Our Communication

Jesus' saving action unfolds in a simple way. He breaks down a wall of separation, one request at a time, one word after another, inviting us into conversation, inviting us to take first a small risk to reveal something of ourselves while he reveals himself. From there he leads us deeper, ever deeper into the mystery of God, into the self-communication of God that creates us and speaks to us. Seated by the well, Jesus recreates the garden where we and God once spoke easily—in a conversation, listening and talking. (page 42)

1. Think of a truly satisfying conversation you have had with another person. What adjectives would you use to describe that conversation: meaningful? pleasant? humorous? personal?

2. Are there persons in your life with whom you find it easy to strike up a conversation? What makes them easier or better conversation partners? Is there a co-worker with whom all communication is blocked or strained? Using the seven characteristics of Jesus' conversation with the Samaritan woman, can you identify the blockage? How could you attempt to begin a conversation with this person?

3. "Jews don't talk with Samaritans." Are there prejudices that keep you from talking to others? Can you identify them and where they come from? What aspects of your life are suffering because of these prejudices? Do others have prejudices against you or stereotypes that block communication? What would be the risk of addressing the person(s) with which communication has been blocked by prejudice?

4. When have you trusted another to disclose your deeper thoughts or feelings? What was that like? Did the other person respect your trust? Was there reciprocal self-disclosure? How did you seek each other's good?

5. In the scriptural account of Jesus' dialogue with the Samaritan woman, we find more than a pattern for good human communication. We discover the way Jesus communicates with us. The process of communication matters to Jesus. He wants to set you free to give voice to what matters most to you. Make time to read prayerfully once more the account from the Gospel of John. In place of the Samaritan woman, substitute your own name.

Allow Jesus to ask you questions that encourage you to risk revealing yourself, to risk trusting him. What have you never told Jesus? What do you wish he knew about you? What are the prejudices you have against Jesus? What do you want Jesus to tell you about himself?

Prayer

Lord,
what a marvel that Jesus shows us
how our communication with you
opens the way for our communication with
     each other,
and that our conversations with one another
open the way for a closer communion with you!
Teach us to have the courage to approach
     one another.
Teach us to have the patience to get to trust
     and to know each other.
Lead us beyond the surface of our conversations
     to those deeper issues:
the loves of our hearts,
the knowledge of you,
the respect we can bear for each other.
Lord, let our conversations with you
become conversations with each other.

CHAPTER FOUR

How Do We Hear *God's* Voice?

Community and Organizational Communication

JOHN 9:1–41

As he walked along, he saw a man blind from birth. His disciples asked him, "Rabbi, who sinned, this man or his parents, that he was born blind?" Jesus answered, "Neither this man nor his parents sinned; he was born blind so that God's works might be revealed in him. We must work the works of him who sent me while it is day; night is coming when no one can work. As long as I am in the world, I am the light of the world." When he had said this, he spat on the ground and made mud with the saliva and spread the mud on the man's eyes, saying to him, "Go, wash in the pool of Siloam" (which means Sent). Then he went and washed and came back able to see.

The neighbors and those who had seen him before as a beggar began to ask, "Is this not the man who used to sit and beg?" Some were saying, "It is he." Others were saying, "No, but it is someone like him." He kept saying, "I am the man." But they kept asking him, "Then how were your eyes opened?" He answered, "The man called Jesus made mud, spread it on my eyes, and said to me, 'Go to Siloam and wash.' Then I went and washed and received my sight." They said to him, "Where is he?" He said, "I do not know."

They brought to the Pharisees the man who had formerly been blind. Now it was a sabbath day when Jesus made the mud and opened his eyes. Then the Pharisees also began to ask him how he had received his sight. He said to them, "He put mud on my eyes. Then I washed, and now I see." Some of the Pharisees said, "This man is not from God, for he does not observe the sabbath." But others said, "How can a man who is a sinner perform such signs?" And they were divided. So they said again to the blind man, "What do you say about him? It was your eyes he opened." He said, "He is a prophet."

The Jews did not believe that he had been blind and had received his sight until they called the parents of the man who had received his sight and asked them, "Is this your son, who you say was born blind? How then does he now see?" His parents answered, "We know that this is our son, and that he was born blind; but we do not know how it is that now he sees, nor do we know who opened his eyes. Ask him; he is of age. He will speak for himself." His parents said this because they were afraid of the Jews; for the Jews had already agreed that anyone who confessed Jesus to be the Messiah would be put out of the synagogue. Therefore his parents said, "He is of age, ask him."

So for the second time they called the man who had been blind, and they said to him, "Give glory to God! We know that this man is a sinner." He answered, "I do not know whether he is a sinner. One thing I do know, that though I was blind, now I see." They said to him, "What did he do to you? How did he open your eyes?" He answered them, "I have told you already, and you would not listen. Why do you want to hear it again? Do you also want to become his disciples?" Then they reviled him, saying, "You are his disciple, but we are disciples of Moses. We know that God has spoken to Moses, but as for this man, we do not know where he comes from." The man answered, "Here is an astonishing thing! You do not know where he comes from, and yet he opened my eyes. We know that God does not listen to sinners, but he does listen to one who worships him and obeys his will. Never since the world began has it been heard that anyone opened the eyes of a person born blind. If this man were not from God, he could do nothing." They answered him, "You were born entirely in sins, and are you trying to teach us?" And they drove him out.

Jesus heard that they had driven him out, and when he found him, he said, "Do you believe in the Son of Man?" He answered, "And who is he, sir? Tell me, so that I may believe in him." Jesus said to him, "You have seen him, and the one speaking with you is he." He said, "Lord, I believe." And he worshiped him. Jesus said, "I came into this world for judgment so that those who do not see may see, and those who do see may become blind." Some of the Pharisees near him heard this and said to him, "Surely we are not blind, are we?" Jesus said to them, "If you were blind, you would not have a sin. But now that you say, 'We see,' your sin remains."

"RABBI, WHO SINNED, THIS MAN or his parents?"
Apparently Jesus and the disciples discussed these
kinds of things frequently. They would ask him about
God's Law, about the kingdom, about things they did
not understand. They entered into a conversation
with Jesus, opening their hearts to him, letting him
call forth something deeper in them, much as we have
seen Jesus evoking new life, living waters, real communication from others like the woman of Samaria.
But even in this seemingly free exchange, communication is not perfect. The blocked communication
that comes from that early mistrust still occurs.

"Rabbi, who sinned, this man or his parents?"
they ask. But Jesus rejects their proposed answer: "It
was not that this man sinned, or his parents, but that
the works of God might be made manifest in him."
The blocked communication occurs here because the
disciples closed off the possible answer. They asked,
but at the same time, they thought they knew: it had
to be one or the other. Here Jesus opens communication by expanding their possibilities.

This scene from the ninth chapter of John's
Gospel is worthy of our consideration because it
teaches us more about how God restores blocked
communication. There is a pattern to God's actions,
as we have seen. First, Jesus reminds us of the impor-

tance of listening to God's voice and leads us to an awareness of all those other voices we hear and of the noise that keeps us from hearing. Then, as God reminds us disciples to listen to Jesus, we become aware of the ways that we fail to listen—to each other and much less to God. Only then do we see how interpersonal communication occurs, watching and listening to the ways Jesus brings about the self-disclosure that allows hearts to speak to hearts. By following his example, we can free each other to such self-disclosure. The conversation between Jesus and the woman of Samaria ends with the woman telling others, sharing the conversation that began with Jesus.

Here, then, is the next stage. And because we, like the disciples, so often don't understand it, the Gospel repeatedly demonstrates the pattern. Yes, a conversation with Jesus occurs, but we—like the disciples— limit the options: either the man or his parents sinned, either the Sabbath or healing is fulfilled, either the Law or the prophet Jesus is right, either the religious leaders or the newly sighted man should be believed.

Two things happen here. First, Jesus opens up the possibilities of understanding not either-or, but something else, in this instance (and perhaps in many others as well) the glory of God. This alone teaches us an important lesson: we block off communication by limiting the possibilities of our understanding. If we learn only this—to look for more options, to look for what God might do—we could communicate so much more freely.

The second lesson is more important. We discover the freedom of God's communication through discussion with each other, through a dialogue in which every voice has a place. In John's Gospel, we hear the disciples, we hear Jesus, we hear the man born blind, we hear the people in the streets, we hear the religious leaders, we hear the man's parents, we hear the Pharisees. All those voices have a place. The understanding of God's glory does not occur immediately, but through the conversa-

If we learn only this—to look for more options, to look for what God might do—we could communicate so much more freely.

tions, through the voices, through the time, his glory *is made* manifest and comprehensible.

Let's start again, this time with the man blind from birth. He lives in a world of sound and touch, not light. Out of the noises and voices around him he feels someone's hands putting mud on his eyes, and he hears a man's voice, "Go, wash in the pool of Siloam."

So he does and he begins to see. But with so many years of depending on sound, it seems plausible that what he hears matters more to him than what he sees. We often find ourselves in the opposite camp: sighted, we attend more to what we see. We don't really listen—something brought to our attention on the mountain of the Transfiguration. Because of that, we should force ourselves to pay more attention to the voices than to the vistas here around Jerusalem. The world of the blind man is a present-tense world, a world of sounds and voices and interactions. It's a world of movement and life. But even with that, he does not understand things right away. His experience leads him to listen to all the voices; we can learn from that. Note that this is not the tempter's voice, a voice of mistrust, but the many voices of people trying to understand.

Immediately the people around him ask who he is, this one who looks like the blind man but who can see. The people trust what they see, not what they hear. He speaks. He tells them how he sees. And then they begin to discuss with each other how this could happen. The religious leaders join the discussion. More sure of their answers, they question how a good work like this healing could happen on the Sabbath. And the discussion goes on. No one of them has the answer, but we draw closer to an answer through the debates. Interestingly, John's Gospel does not silence the wrong answers but lets them find a voice. Through the voices, we discover God's glory. Jesus directs the strongest criticism here to those who would cut off the discussion, stopping its flow, and freezing things. When we stop the possibility of hearing others' voices, we also stop the possibility of hearing Jesus' voice. It's the tempter who would substitute one voice of mistrust for the voice of God.

This fact deserves our attention. We discover God's glory through the give-and-take of the voices. With the man once blind, we listen carefully, responding, telling what we have experienced ("He put mud on my eyes and told me to wash. Now I see.") and debating the meaning ("He's a prophet." "He's a sinner." "He comes from God.").

We find ourselves in much the same position. We want to see, we want to know God's glory, we want to understand our experience. The way to do that, the Gospel tells us, lies in listening to the voices, to our dialogue with others. "Faith comes through hearing," Paul tells us, and that hearing involves discussion. We come to faith and to understanding by talking things over. Now such talking demands a willingness really to listen to others. We may not have the answers (or, like the disciples, we may not even have the question right). We may move too quickly to a condemnation (like the Pharisees and religious leaders). The blocked communication becomes unblocked precisely in the riskiness of discussion. Jesus does not absent himself from this discussion, nor does he cut others off from the discussion. He warns the Pharisees and us of the consequences of our cutting others off from it—if we insist too much on our perspective, then we remain in our guilt.

John's Gospel underlines the importance of conversation and dialogue in coming to faith. This provides a model for us at home, in our parishes, in the programs of sacramental preparation, in all sectors of our Church, in government, and in society. We cannot fear the voices of the discussion; we cannot silence those that make us uncomfortable. God's truth emerges and the process of arriving at that truth matters. If we silence voices in the discussion, they do not go away; we only block the possibility of communication and go back to the condition we wish to escape.

The process of discussion forms us into a communion, a community of the word. We need to talk about what we believe and how we believe. That community-forming process never ends. To switch from the ongoing world of voices to the snapshot of an image of the truth attempts to stop a living thing. We end up blind even to that which we think we see.

God's self-communication does not stop. When we think it does, we come face to face with a blocked communication.

By now we should understand at least one thing: our response to one another's communication closely mirrors our response to God's self-communication. If we

If we cannot listen to one another, we cannot listen to God.

cannot listen to one another, we cannot listen to God. If we choose to listen to the tempter's voice, undermining our communication through mistrust, we will mistrust God. If we would stop the discussion that builds up our community of believers, we will block our ears to God's self-communication as well.

When the once-blind man had sorted through God's self-communication in his experience ("He must be from God"), Jesus finds him and speaks with him again, inviting a profession of faith. This is the confidence of our communities, that in the face of all doubts, debates, conversations, God still wants to communicate with us. And he will.

Deepening Our Communication

The discussion goes on. No one of them has the answer, but we draw closer to an answer through the debates. Interestingly, John's Gospel does not silence the wrong answers but lets them find a voice. Through the voices, we discover God's glory. Jesus directs the strongest criticism here to those who would cut off the discussion, stopping its flow, and freezing things. When we stop the possibility of hearing others' voices, we also stop the possibility of hearing Jesus' voice. It's the tempter who would substitute one voice of mistrust for the voice of God. (page 55)

1. Think about an issue, policy, or decision attracting a lot of attention in your own life or in the public forum. Whose are the loudest voices in the discussion? Can you think of perspectives or possibilities that have not been voiced? If you're a woman, ask how a man would view it; if a man, ask how a woman would see it. If you are an adult, ask how a child would see it. If you are a Catholic, ask how a Muslim would see it. If you are a "liberal," ask how a "conservative" would view it, etc. Can you take one more step and discuss it with someone who has a

different viewpoint than your own, seeking to understand the other's perspective? What is this like? Write down the feelings that come up during the conversation. How do these feelings affect your listening? Your speaking?

2. Think of a time when you couldn't understand someone. What does your culture/ nation/church/politics/family contribute to that limited vision? How do "the usual ways of thinking" block your communication?

3. In family/group communication settings, is there someone who does not get to speak? What voices do we tend to ignore or discount? Why? Whose voice is not heard in political discourse? In discussion of religious issues?

4. In the Scripture reading, each person in the dialogue had a different image of God, and through the discussion each was invited to see God in a new way. What is your image of God? Have others challenged you to expand this image? Are there times when you have felt resistance to this? Where does the resistance come from? What has happened when you took in new perspectives of God?

Prayer

Dear Lord,
the world seems so complicated,
and there are days when we want simple answers.
Keep us from acting as though we know all
    the answers,
as though we can limit what we and others
    can or should say.
Teach us to listen even to those we'd rather
    not hear.
Give us a sensitivity to word and sound,
that we might hear as you hear.
Give us a sense of discernment.
Give us a renewed ability to see
that we might see as you see.
Give us a sense of openness.
Make us people of your word and your vision.

CHAPTER FIVE

Will Fear Keep Us from Listening?

When Communicating Feels Like Death

JOHN 11:1–44

Now a certain man was ill, Lazarus of Bethany, the village of Mary and her sister Martha. Mary was the one who anointed the Lord with perfume and wiped his feet with her hair; her brother Lazarus was ill.

So the sisters sent a message to Jesus, "Lord, he whom you love is ill." But when Jesus heard it, he said, "This illness does not lead to death; rather it is

for God's glory, so that the Son of God may be glo-
rified through it." Accordingly, though Jesus loved
Martha and her sister and Lazarus, after having
heard that Lazarus was ill, he stayed two days longer
in the place where he was.

Then after this he said to the disciples, "Let us go
to Judea again." The disciples said to him, "Rabbi,
the Jews were just now trying to stone you, and are
you going there again?" Jesus answered, "Are there
not twelve hours of daylight? Those who walk during the day do not stumble, because they see the
light of this world. But those who walk at night
stumble, because the light is not in them." After saying this, he told them, "Our friend Lazarus has fall-
en asleep, but I am going there to awaken him." The
disciples said to him, "Lord, if he has fallen asleep, he
will be all right." Jesus, however, had been speaking
about his death, but they thought that he was refer-
ring merely to sleep. Then Jesus told them plainly,
"Lazarus is dead. For your sake I am glad I was not
there, so that you may believe. But let us go to him."
Thomas, who was called the Twin, said to his fellow
disciples, "Let us also go, that we may die with him."

When Jesus arrived, he found that Lazarus had
already been in the tomb four days. Now Bethany
was near Jerusalem, some two miles away, and many
of the Jews had come to Martha and Mary to con-
sole them about their brother. When Martha heard
that Jesus was coming, she went and met him, while

Mary stayed at home. Martha said to Jesus, "Lord, if you had been here, my brother would not have died. But even now I know that God will give you whatever you ask of him." Jesus said to her, "Your brother will rise again." Martha said to him, "I know that he will rise again in the resurrection on the last day." Jesus said to her, "I am the resurrection and the life. Those who believe in me, even though they die, will live, and everyone who lives and believes in me will never die. Do you believe this?" She said to him, "Yes, Lord; I believe that you are the Messiah, the Son of God, the one coming into the world."

When she had said this, she went back and called her sister Mary, and told her privately, "The Teacher is here and is calling for you." And when she heard it, she got up quickly and went to him. Now Jesus had not yet come to the village, but was still at the place where Martha had met him. The Jews who were with her in the house, consoling her, saw Mary get up quickly and go out. They followed her because they thought that she was going to the tomb to weep there. When Mary came where Jesus was and saw him, she knelt at his feet and said to him, "Lord, if you had been here, my brother would not have died." When Jesus saw her weeping, and the Jews who came with her also weeping, he greatly disturbed in spirit and deeply moved. He said, "Where have you laid him?" They said to him, "Lord, come and see."

Jesus began to weep. So the Jews said, "See how he loved him!" But some of them said, "Could not he who opened the eyes of the blind man have kept this man from dying?"

Then Jesus, again greatly disturbed, came to the tomb. It was a cave, and a stone was lying against it. Jesus said, "Take away the stone." Martha, the sister of the dead man, said to him, "Lord, already there is a stench because he has been dead four days." Jesus said to her, "Did I not tell you that if you believed, you would see the glory of God?" So they took away the stone. And Jesus looked upward and said, "Father, I thank you for having heard me. I knew that you always hear me, but I have said this for the sake of the crowd standing here, so that they may believe that you have sent me." When he had said this, he cried with a loud voice, "Lazarus, come out." The dead man came out, his hands and feet bound with strips of cloth, and his face wrapped in a cloth. Jesus said to them, "Unbind him, and let him go."

Once again we must begin with the knowledge that God wants to communicate with us. This is something we've come to know at each stage of these reflections. And, at the same time, as we examine our consciences, we also recognize that we turn from God's voice: we listen to other voices; we drown out his word with our own talking; we erect barriers to communication; we block off the possibility of communication by placing limits on it or refusing to enter the play of searching voices.

God's action is always to take the initiative, to open up communication, to speak a word to us.

But God's action is always to take the initiative, to open up communication, to speak a word to us. We hear this story again, but now the story acts as a kind of climax. God's word addresses us at the very center of our refusal to communicate. His word speaks in the place where we seem to cut ourselves off from communication most dramatically—death. It's not called the silence of the tomb for nothing.

Lazarus is dead. Jesus tells the disciples, since they have misunderstood death. Like all of us, they would rather not think of death, they would rather sugarcoat it, taking Jesus' metaphorical reference to Lazarus' falling asleep as literal. We think we know better: we can acknowledge the sleep of death, we think. But we, like the disciples, would rather hide from the reality of death. Death. Silence. Isolation. Death represents the final refusal of communication. We don't just stop our ears, blocking sound. In death, we enter into silence, cut off from everyone.

It's not a thing,
this resurrection,
but it is a person.
It is a relationship with
that person.
It is a love
and a love
that communicates.

The frightening thing here is that in some ways we would choose this silence. No one can break through now. It's the logical conclusion to our suspicions of communication, to the blockages we erect. If the sin isolates us, then death merely completes the action. If we would block out each other's voices and God's voice with them, then we are indeed dead.

The refusal to communicate cuts even the living. We've already seen that one way in which we turn from God's communication is to listen to other voices. Even those who love Jesus do that. The visitors asked how it was that Jesus, who healed the man who was blind, could not have healed Lazarus and prevented his death. Martha and Mary listen to that voice. Martha greets Jesus with, "Master, if you had been here my brother would not have died." She listens to the tempter's voice, the one that says, "Can you really trust God?"

In the face of this, Jesus speaks two words. In them we hear God's self-communication.

Jesus' first word addresses the living, and, with Martha, we hear it. She is distraught, she is torn by grief, she is bereft. We, like her, stand similarly in the face of death: shocked, alone, surprised, saddened, angry, exhausted. When we stand before another's death, we contemplate our own. We long to hear any voice that speaks...or sometimes none at all. The communication we welcome is that of the most elementary kind: a touch, a presence. We live in a kind of isolation, exactly in the situation of blocked communication.

Then Jesus speaks. "He will rise again."

Mary answers in a pro forma way. "Yes, on the last day" (whenever and whatever that is). She begins to respond to God's promise. "I know," she says, as she has learned from the Scriptures.

Jesus speaks again. "I am the resurrection." God's self-communication works to invite Martha, Mary, and us to faith. Jesus invites us to trust God's word. Jesus invites Martha, then Mary, then us into a relationship. It's not a thing, this resurrection, but it is a person. It is a relationship with that person. It's a love and a love that communicates. As long as we are in this relationship, we know the resurrection. It's interesting that Jesus begins with the invitation to faith. Then it becomes evident—faith is the relationship: we can only hear God if we are willing to trust God.

*We can only
hear God
if we are willing
to trust God.*

Martha responds in the way that should be familiar to us now. She hears God's self-communication, and she goes to tell others. She brings her sister. But Mary, too overcome by grief, cannot hear God's word through Martha. Jesus speaks. But this time the invitation to trust is phrased in the simple desire to accompany Mary and Martha.

The second word that Jesus speaks, addresses Lazarus. "Lazarus, come out."

He calls him by name.

And in the moment of that call, we enter into a moment where time begins. It is God's moment, the moment of the creation. God said, "Let there be life." And there was life.

Jesus calls Lazarus by name. God's word of address is his self-communication.

It echoes in the silence of the tomb, in the silence of death, in the place where we take refuge from God. It reaches out to us in our refusal to be in his presence.

God's self-communication calls us by name.

And in that moment between death and life, God's word is alive and active.

Lazarus walks out of the tomb into a world created anew by God's word.

"Untie him and let him go," Jesus says. When communication is restored, the bonds are released and human community can begin. Lazarus...not alone, not Lazarus and Jesus alone, but Lazarus, Jesus, Martha, and Mary...and their friends.

And yet, this self-communication of God is not without cost. John tells us just a few verses later that Jesus' words and actions will lead directly to his death.

We fear God's word, and, in our sinfulness, in our move toward death, we would block it out, build barriers against it, stop our ears, listen anywhere else. The challenge for us now is to ask ourselves, "Why?" If God's self-communication is the word of life, why do we resist it? Do we so desire life on our terms that we do not even want to hear his word of life? That we would rather choose the silence of death?

Deepening Our Communication

Jesus speaks again. "I am the resurrection." God's self-communication works to invite Martha, Mary, and us to faith. Jesus invites us to trust God's word. Jesus invites Martha, then Mary, then us into a relationship. It's not a thing, this resurrection, but it is a person. It is a relationship with that person. It's a love and a love that communicates. As long as we are in this relationship, we know the resurrection. It's interesting that Jesus begins with the invitation to faith. Then it becomes evident—faith is the relationship: we can only hear God if we are willing to trust God. (page 67)

1. Have there been times when someone told you things you didn't want to hear? Or times when someone tried to explain something to you that you just couldn't understand? Or has someone told you something that changed your life? How did you respond in each case? How are each of these situations like faith?

2. Have you ever been in a situation in which there was no human possibility for resolution and *the only thing left* was to trust God? What was this moment of faith like? How

did it affect your relationship with God? With others?

3. What is your idea of a "good life"? Do you have any cherished dreams? How do you talk to God about these desires? Or do you try to keep them "hidden" from him, attempting to make them come true by yourself? Have there been times when you've said to God, "If only you had...?" How did he respond?

4. In the Scripture reading, Jesus personally addresses each person: Martha, Mary, Lazarus. At this moment, to which of these three persons do you relate the most? Why? In a time of quiet prayer, allow Jesus to come to you and address you by name. What is it like to hear Jesus call you by name? What does he have to say to you right now?

Prayer

Dear God,
we want to live,
but so often we choose not to live.
We want to hear you,
but so often we choose to listen to other voices.
Please call our name.
Give us again to one another.
May your Son's prayer be fulfilled in us:
that we may be in you as he is in you.
May we know your life
as we hear your voice.

CHAPTER SIX

How Do We Respond to Hostility?

Communicating through Silence and Truth

MATTHEW 26:31–27, 61

Then Jesus said to them, "You will become deserters because of me this night; for it is written, 'I will strike the shepherd, and the sheep of the flock will be scattered.' But after I am raised up, I will go ahead of you to Galilee." Peter said to him, "Though all become deserters because of you, I will never desert you." Jesus said to him, "Truly I tell you, this very night, before the cock crows, you will deny me three times." Peter said to him, "Even though I must die with you, I will not deny you." And so said all the disciples.

Then Jesus went with them to a place called Gethsemane; and he said to his disciples, "Sit here while I go over there and pray." He took with him Peter and the two sons of Zebedee and began to be grieved and agitated. Then he said to them, "I am deeply grieved, even to death; remain here, and stay awake with me." And going a little farther, he threw himself on the ground and prayed, "My Father, if it be possible, let this cup pass from me; yet not what I want but what you want." Then he came to the disciples and found them sleeping; and he said to Peter, "So, could you not stay awake with me one hour? Stay awake and pray that you may not come into the time of trial; the spirit indeed is willing, but the flesh is weak." Again he went away for the second time and prayed, "My Father, if this cannot pass unless I drink it, your will be done." Again he came and found them sleeping, for their eyes were heavy. So leaving them again, he went away and prayed for the third time, saying the same words. Then he came to the disciples and said to them, "Are you still sleeping and taking your rest? See, the hour is at hand, and the Son of Man is betrayed into the hands of sinners. Get up, let us be going. See, my betrayer is at hand."

While he was still speaking, Judas, one of the twelve, arrived; with him was a large crowd with swords and clubs, from the chief priests and the elders of the people. Now the betrayer had given them a sign, saying, "The one I will kiss is the man; arrest him." At once he came up to Jesus and said, "Greetings, Rabbi!" and kissed him. Jesus said to him, "Friend, do what you are here to do." Then they came and laid hands on Jesus and arrested him. Suddenly, one of those with Jesus put his hand on his sword, drew it, and struck the slave of the high priest, cutting off his ear. Then Jesus said to him, "Put your sword back into its place; for all who take the sword will perish by the sword. Do you think that I cannot appeal to my Father, and he will at once send me more than twelve legions of angels? But how then would the scriptures be fulfilled, which say it must happen in this way?" At that hour Jesus said to the crowds, "Have you come out with swords and clubs to arrest me as though I were a bandit? Day after day I sat in the temple teaching, and you did not arrest me. But all this has taken place, so that the scriptures of the prophets may be fulfilled." Then all the disciples deserted him and fled.

Those who had arrested Jesus took him to Caiaphas the high priest, in whose house the scribes and the elders had gathered. But Peter was following him at a distance, as far as the courtyard of the high priest; and going inside, he sat with the guards in order to see how this would end. Now the chief priests and the whole council were looking for false testimony against Jesus so that they might put him to death, but they found none, though many false witnesses came forward. At last two came forward and said, "This fellow said, 'I am able to destroy the temple of God and to build it in three days.'" The high priest stood up and said, "Have you no answer? What is it that they testify against you?" But Jesus was silent. Then the high priest said to him, "I put you under oath before the living God, tell us if you are the Messiah, the Son of God." Jesus said to him, "You have said so. But I tell you, from now on you will see the Son of Man seated at the right hand of Power and coming on the clouds of heaven." Then the high priest tore his clothes and said, "He has blasphemed! Why do we still need witnesses? You have now heard his blasphemy. What is your verdict?" They answered, "He deserves death." Then they spat in his face and struck him; and some slapped him, saying, "Prophesy to us, you Messiah! Who is it that struck you?"

Now Peter was sitting outside in the courtyard. A servant-girl came to him and said, "You also were with Jesus the Galilean." But he denied it before them all, saying, "I do not know what you are talking about." When he went out to the porch, another servant-girl saw him, and she said to the bystanders,

"This man was with Jesus of Nazareth." Again he denied it with an oath, "I do not know the man." After a little while the bystanders came up and said to Peter, "Certainly you are also one of them, for your accent betrays you." Then he began to curse, and he swore an oath, "I do not know the man!" At that moment the cock crowed. Then Peter remembered what Jesus had said, "Before the cock crows, you will deny me three times." And he went out and wept bitterly.

When morning came, all the chief priests and the elders of the people conferred together against Jesus in order to bring about his death. They bound him, led him away, and handed him over to Pilate the governor.

When Judas, his betrayer, saw that Jesus was condemned, he repented and brought back the thirty pieces of silver to the chief priests and the elders. He said, "I have sinned by betraying innocent blood." But they said, "What is that to us? See to it yourself." Throwing down the pieces of silver in the temple, he departed; and he went and hanged himself. But the chief priests, taking the pieces of silver, said, "It is not lawful to put them into the treasury, since they are blood money." After conferring together, they used them to buy the potter's field as a place to bury foreigners. For this reason that field has been called the Field of Blood to this day. Then was fulfilled what had been spoken through the prophet Jeremiah, "And they took the thirty pieces of silver, the price of the one on whom a price had been set, on whom some of the people of Israel had set a price, and they gave them for the potter's field, as the Lord commanded me."

Now Jesus stood before the governor; and the governor asked him, "Are you the King of the Jews?" Jesus said, "You say so." But when he was accused by the chief priests and elders, he did not answer. Then Pilate said to him, "Do you not hear how many accusations they make against you?" But he gave him no answer, not even to a single charge, so that the governor was greatly amazed.

Now at the festival the governor was accustomed to release a prisoner for the crowd, anyone whom they wanted. At that time they had a notorious prisoner, called Jesus Barabbas. So after they had gathered, Pilate said to them, "Whom do you want me to release for you, Jesus Barabbas or Jesus who is called the Messiah?" For he realized that it was out of jealousy that they had handed him over. While he was sitting on the judgment seat, his wife sent word to him, "Have nothing to do with that innocent man, for today I have suffered a great deal because of a dream about him." Now the chief priests and the elders persuaded the crowds to ask for Barabbas and to have Jesus killed. The governor again said to them, "Which of the two do you want me to release for you?" And they said, "Barabbas." Pilate said to them, "Then what should I do with Jesus who is called the Messiah?" All of them said, "Let him be crucified!" Then he asked, "Why, what evil has he done?" But they shouted all the more, "Let him be crucified!"

So when Pilate saw that he could do nothing, but rather that a riot was beginning, he took some water and washed his hands before the crowd, saying, "I am innocent of this man's blood; see to it yourselves." Then the people as a whole answered, "His blood be on us and on our children!" So he released Barabbas for them; and after flogging Jesus, he handed him over to be crucified.

Then the soldiers of the governor took Jesus into the governor's headquarters, and they gathered the whole cohort around him. They stripped him and put a scarlet robe on him, and after twisting some thorns into a crown, they put it on his head. They put a reed in his right hand and knelt before him and mocked him, saying, "Hail, King of the Jews!" They spat on him, and took the reed and struck him on the head. After mocking him, they stripped him of the robe and put his own clothes on him. Then they led him away to crucify him.

As they went out, they came upon a man from Cyrene named Simon; they compelled this man to carry his cross. And when they came to a place called Golgotha (which means Place of a Skull), they offered him wine to drink, mixed with gall; but when he tasted it, he would not drink it. And when they had crucified him, they divided his clothes among themselves by casting lots; then they sat down there and kept watch over him. Over his head they put the charge against him, which read, "This is Jesus, the King of the Jews."

Then two bandits were crucified with him, one on his right and one on his left. Those who passed by derided him, shaking their heads and saying, "You who would destroy the temple and build it in three days, save yourself! If you are the Son of God, come down from the cross." In the same way the chief priests also, along with the scribes and elders, were mocking him, saying, "He saved others; he cannot save himself. He is the King of Israel; let him come down from the cross now, and we will believe in him. He trusts in God; let God deliver him now, if he wants to; for he said, 'I am God's Son.'" The bandits who were crucified with him also taunted him in the same way.

From noon on, darkness came over the whole land until three in the afternoon. And about three o'clock Jesus cried with a loud voice, "Eli, Eli, lama sabachthani?" that is, "My God, my God, why have you forsaken me?" When some of the bystanders heard it, they said, "This man is calling for Elijah." At once one of them ran and got a sponge, filled it with sour wine, put it on a stick, and gave it to him to drink. But the others said, "Wait, let us see whether Elijah will come to save him." Then Jesus cried again with a loud voice and breathed his last. At that moment the curtain of the temple was torn in two, from top to bottom. The earth shook, and the rocks were split. The tombs also were opened, and many bodies of the saints who had fallen asleep were raised. After his resurrection they came out of the tombs and entered the holy city and appeared to many. Now when the centurion and those with him, who were keeping watch over Jesus, saw the earthquake and what took place, they were terrified and said, "Truly this man was God's Son!"

Many women were also there, looking on from a distance; they had followed Jesus from Galilee and had provided for him. Among them were Mary Magdalene, and Mary the mother of James and Joseph, and the mother of the sons of Zebedee.

When it was evening, there came a rich man from Arimathea, named Joseph, who was also a disciple of Jesus. He went to Pilate and asked for the body of Jesus; then Pilate ordered it to be given to him. So Joseph took the body and wrapped it in a clean linen cloth and laid it in his own new tomb, which he had hewn in the rock. He then rolled a great stone to the door of the tomb and went away. Mary Magdalene and the other Mary were there, sitting opposite the tomb.

GOD ALWAYS TAKES THE INITIATIVE to communicate with us, overcoming even the blocked communication that so characterizes our living. What characterizes God's communication?

The death of Jesus demonstrates in a powerful way God's communication and recapitulates the ways that Jesus opens communication. Rereading the account of his death we can highlight the two key aspects of Jesus' communication: silence in response to mockery, and truth as the last word.

Silence: Jesus' Response to Mockery

First, Jesus responds to blocked communication by silence in the face of the destructive lie. He denies the power of mockery. In his dying, Jesus faces this mockery three times: the mocking at his trial before the high priest, the mocking by the Roman soldiers, and the mocking by the priests, bystanders, and criminals at the cross.

At the trial, the accusations mix with derision, *"Then they spat in his face and struck him; and some slapped him, saying, 'Prophesy to us, you Messiah! Who is it that struck you?'"* What is this but the human use of communication to torture another? We choose words precisely to hurt, to cut off any possibility of connection. The mocking isn't necessary in the trial, but it serves to place a distance between Jesus and the others.

The Roman soldiers mock Jesus in a twofold way: verbally and nonverbally. *"Hail, King of the Jews!"* They *"put a scarlet robe on him, and after twisting some thorns into a crown, they put it on his head. They put a reed in his right hand...."* Coming from members of an occupying power, their mocking reflects not just a contempt for Jesus but a contempt for the people of Israel. But the purpose is the same. Mocking creates distance, cuts one group off from another, rein-

God always takes the initiative to communicate with us.

forces an in-group identity. This other person, these other people are not fit for our communication.

At Calvary, all the characters seem to mock Jesus. Stripped of all—clothes, dignity, freedom, movement—Jesus hears the taunts. In their eyes, he is nothing, cut off from all communication. Nailed to the cross, excluded from their interaction, seemingly, he can only hear. The mockery—all mockery—deliberately prevents communication by using language to separate rather than to join. Ironically and perversely, mocking cannot work without joining with the power of words. It destroys the very thing that it depends on. Mocking contradicts language, contradicts communication.

The mocking at the death of Jesus marks the death of communication as well.

All of us know the power of mockery. To be brutally honest, we've both experienced it and done it to others. We take our language, our words, and use them to build walls—the angry words that signal our preference not to talk; the twisting jokes that make a person an object; the deliberate misinterpretation to gain a laugh at the expense of someone else; the slight change of meaning for our advantage at work. In big and small ways, we use the facility of a common language—that which makes us one—into something that isolates others and, if we think about it, ourselves as well.

Making fun of others destroys communication. We do it almost gleefully in playgrounds, on talk shows, in hallways, in political debates, at parties, and in homes.

The mockery at the death of Jesus marks the death of communication as well. As we share in it, we share in that death of communication.

And so the mocking represents something else, too—something else we've seen before. The mocking at the trial, in the prison, on the hill all represent another voice, the same other voice that seduced Adam and Eve. "Can you trust God?" it asked. "Did God really say not to...?" This voice asks, "Can you trust us?"

Jesus' response to this mockery teaches us yet one more time how God restores broken communication. Jesus remains silent.

Where communication is perverted, where what should join separates, Jesus responds by not acknowledging the lie. To respond, to acknowledge means participating in the destruction of language. So Jesus remains silent, and, silent, he upholds (among other things) the dignity of communication. He communicates, as he always does, by giving himself in love to others, but he does not honor the mocking lie. We see and hear that in his action and in the words he does speak.

Truth: The Last Word

In the midst of mockery and lies, Jesus does have a last word.

Jesus tells the truth. He always tells the truth, no matter how threatening, unpleasant, or politically dangerous. When he has his last meal with the disciples—even before he shares his most intimate moment with them, offering his life, his Body and

Blood for them and to them—even then, he tells them that one of them will betray him. That truth shocks and dismays them, but he speaks the truth to them. It's a truth he speaks to us as well because we too need to know that we will betray him (perhaps in

Jesus always tells the truth, no matter how threatening, unpleasant, or politically dangerous.

ways rather smaller than larger, but betrayal nonetheless). Even then, he will offer his life, his Body and Blood for us and to us. It's a truth of God's nature, a truth of love. But it is the truth: each one of us will betray him.

Then, in the midst of their profession of loyalty, when Peter, the leader, the impetuous, the generous, the insightful, when this Peter professes a willingness to die for him (and he *will* die for him), Jesus tells him that even in his good-heartedness, Peter will deny him, not once but three times. He tells him the truth: his fear will cast out his loyalty. Once again, Jesus speaks that truth not just to Peter but also to all the disciples and to us. Even in our following of Jesus, no matter how wholehearted, we, like Peter, will at times deny him. And yet Jesus still feeds Peter; he still brings him to watch and pray with him; he still looks at him with love. He tells Peter the truth.

At prayer, Jesus tells the truth of his desires and of his heart. "Father, let this cup pass from me." It's a terrible thing before him: betrayal, denial, judgment, shame, torture, death. Of course he wishes some other way. He tells the truth. It's a truth that we recognize more quickly than many others, for we feel the same. We, too, wish that God's will would not lead us to suffering or sacrifice or inconvenience or the pain of love. We know this truth.

And then he tells the truth of his relationship to the Father. "But not my will but yours be done." The truth of his relationship with his Father runs deeper than the truth of his desires, of his fears, of his thoughts. The truth is this: the Father's will is paramount; the truth is summed up in the words: "Let your will be done." Here is a truth that we long to know: a truth of trust in God, the truth of a relationship with God, the truth of a love.

Arrested, arraigned before the religious leaders and later before Pilate, Jesus tells the truth. "You will see the Son of Man on the clouds of heaven." "Are you a king?" "You say it." This truth seems to mark him as politically naive, but he speaks the truth. He cannot do otherwise. If God would restore communication, unblock it, undo the tempter's planted suspicions, then truth alone will do. God's word is trustworthy because God's Word is trustworthy

Finally, Jesus speaks the truth in the face of death, even to his Father. "My God, my God, why have you forsaken me?" He dies as we all must do. Entering into that silence, that last blocked communication, he tells the truth of our human experience. We feel alone. We feel cut off. We feel forsaken. He speaks the truth, one last time, "My God, my God, why have you forsaken me?"

The truth is that we can trust God. Telling God the truth banishes suspicion and brings trust.

Tell God the truth.

Here again is how God restores broken communication. The truth rebuilds trust by "chancing" it—by taking the chance that another can be trusted, by placing trust in the other. The truth is that we can trust God. Telling God the truth banishes suspicion and brings trust.

And, as we trust God, we begin the journey of trusting each other.

Deepening Our Communication

Here again is how God restores broken communication. The truth rebuilds trust by "chancing" it—by taking the chance that another can be trusted, by placing trust in the other. The truth is that we can trust God. Telling God the truth banishes suspicion and brings trust. And, as we trust God, we begin the journey of trusting each other. (page 88)

1. Is there a situation in your life where words are being used to mock? To misinterpret for personal advantage? To laugh at the expense of others? How can you make a difference by authentic communion, by, like Jesus, giving yourself in love?

2. We, like Peter, have to know that we will betray Jesus. And we also need to know, like Peter, that Jesus will still feed us and look on us with love. It is our truth. It is God's truth. Reflecting on this truth, what is aroused in your heart? To what commitment are you being drawn?

3. Have their been times when you have begged God to be rescued from something painful or

shameful? Were you able to say, "Not my will
but yours be done"? What do you think about
the "will of God"? Do you feel that God is
trustworthy? Why or why not? Has he been
trustworthy in your life?

4. When have you told God the truth, letting
   him know how you honestly feel? What
   happened? How does doing this amount to
   "chancing" that God can be trusted? Can
   you talk about a time when you had to take
   a great risk to trust another person? How did
   you change or grow as a result? How did
   your relationship change or grow?

5. In the Scripture reading, Jesus' communication
   with Peter shows us how God communicates.
   Jesus' communication is honest, loving, reli-
   able. He offers his life, his Body and his Blood
   for Peter and for us. How would you charac-
   terize God's communication with you? Like
   Peter, have you begun to hear more of what
   God is saying to you in your daily life?

Prayer

Father,

with Jesus, we cry out to you.

We know how broken our communication is.

Almost every day we experience those things

that hurt us and isolate us.

Let us follow Jesus in silence where silence matters.

Let us follow Jesus in truth in all things.

Let us begin by telling you the truth:

    how we long for you,

    how we long for each other,

    how afraid we are,

    how alone we feel.

Give us Jesus.

Give us Jesus as companion and guide,

as word and Word.

Give us Jesus as truth.

Give us Jesus in silence.

Give us Jesus.

Give us Jesus.

CHAPTER SEVEN

Jesus Tells Us, "Be Not Afraid!"

Communication Restored

JOHN 20:1–18

Early on the first day of the week, while it was still dark, Mary Magdalene came to the tomb and saw that the stone had been removed from the tomb. So she ran and went to Simon Peter and the other disciple, the one whom Jesus loved, and said to them, "They have taken the Lord out of the tomb, and we do not know where they have laid him." Then Peter and the other disciple set out and went toward the tomb. The two were running together, but the other disciple outran Peter and reached the tomb first. He bent down to look in and saw the linen wrappings lying there, but he did not go in. Then Simon Peter came, following him, and went into the tomb. He saw the linen wrappings lying there, and the cloth that had been on Jesus' head, not lying with the linen wrappings but rolled up in a place by itself. Then the other disciple, who reached the tomb first, also went in, and he saw and believed; for as yet they did not understand the scripture, that he must rise from the dead. Then the disciples returned to their homes.

But Mary stood weeping outside the tomb. As she wept, she bent over to look into the tomb; and she saw two angels in white, sitting where the body of Jesus had been lying, one at the head and the other at the feet. They said to her, "Woman, why are you weeping?" She said to them, "They have taken away my Lord, and I do not know where they have laid him." When she had said this, she turned around and saw Jesus standing there, but she did not know that it was Jesus.

Jesus said to her, "Woman, why are you weeping? Whom are you looking for?" Supposing him to be the gardener, she said to him, "Sir, if you have carried him away, tell me where you have laid him, and I will take him away." Jesus said to her, "Mary!" She turned and said to him in Hebrew, "Rabboni!" (which means Teacher). Jesus said to her, "Do not hold on to me, because I have not yet ascended to the Father. But go to my brothers and say to them, 'I am ascending to my Father and your Father, to my God and your God.'" Mary Magdalene went and announced to the disciples, "I have seen the Lord"; and she told them that he had said these things to her.

BUT, NO MATTER HOW IMPORTANT are the silence and truth of the cross, the story does not end with them.

What began in a garden begins again in a garden.

And it begins in the simplest way. Panicked, grief-stricken, she weeps, and he asks why. *"Sir, if you have carried him away, tell me where you have laid him, and I will take him away."*

Jesus, who is God's Word, that is, God's restoration of communication, acts definitively. "Mary," he says. He calls her by name. And, called by name, she recognizes the voice—or rather, recognizes herself in the naming. "Mary." God restores communication by giving us a name, but only after listening to us. Jesus listens Mary into existence. Jesus, even supposed to be the gardener, hears, listens, calls, names. And it works. For, given a name, Mary lives and speaks in a relationship with God. "Those who hear my words," Jesus says, "have eternal life" (Jn 5:24).

Mary understands, too. "Rabboni." She listens to her own name and reciprocates—gives Jesus a name, listens to Jesus.

When you are afraid, listen to the voice of God, the voice that says, "Don't be afraid."

There is, then, a second aspect to God's communication, to God's unblocking of communication. Jesus rises.

Once again he will meet the disciples: the women and men who love him, who follow him. The relationships formed throughout his life have not ended, as he sends Mary to tell them.

And, meeting them, Jesus greets the Eleven in the same way that he greets Mary, "Don't be afraid."

Here is the complement to Jesus' listening and naming, the fulfillment of God's reestablishment of communication. "Don't be afraid." Don't hide as Eve and Adam did, out of fear. Don't cower before God's voice as Peter, James, and John did so fearfully on the mountain. Don't fence yourselves off from one another in fear as did the Jews and Samaritans. Don't blind yourselves by fearing how you might misunderstand God's love and law, as did those around the man born blind. Don't let grief terrify you as it did Martha and Mary. Don't be afraid.

If you would share in the open communication that God wishes, don't be afraid.

When you are afraid, listen to the voice of God, the voice that says, "Don't be afraid."

God wants to communicate with us. What God wants to communicate is nothing less than God's very self, a giving of self in love.

God wants to communicate with us, but like all communication, it takes two. God won't force us, but God does want to communicate with us.

And God wants us to communicate with each other at every level, as we have seen and pondered in our hearts. We have watched and heard as God restores communication by calling us by name, by telling and hearing the truth, by addressing us even when we think we are cut off from life, by opening the possibilities of understanding, by opening us to discussion of unexpected points of view, by breaking down the barriers of separation, by taking away our fear.

God urges us and teaches us to set aside suspicion, to learn to trust.

In all of this God tells us, "Don't be afraid."

Deepening Our Communication

God wants us to communicate with each other at every level, as we have seen and pondered in our hearts. We have watched and heard as God restores communication by calling us by name, by telling and hearing the truth, by addressing us even when we think we are cut off from all life, by opening the possibilities of understanding, by opening us to discussion of unexpected points of view, by breaking down the barriers of separation, by taking away our fear. God urges us and teaches us to set aside suspicion, to learn to trust. (page 97)

1. "Jesus *listens* Mary into existence." What have you been saying to God recently? How has your conversation with him affected your life? What is different about your life now? Your faith? What changes when God calls you by name?

2. Are you afraid of God? If so, how does this fear affect your life? What would be different if you knew deeply God's love for you?

3. What are the places or aspects of your life where you feel cut off from life? How is God working to restore the broken communication? To what is he drawing you?

4. In the Scripture passage, take the place of
    Mary looking for Jesus. Imagine yourself in
    the garden, the place where communication
    is finally restored, the place where Jesus
    comes looking for you, the place where
    Jesus listens and speaks to your heart, the
    place where you are called by name. Allow
    God to communicate to you very deeply, to
    communicate to you his very self, to tell you
    how greatly you are understood and loved.
    Bring with you into the garden any persons
    with whom communication is broken. Jesus
    breaks down the separation between you.
    Feel him removing your fear of each other.
    At the end of this book, how has your com-
    munication been renewed? Spend some time
    in profound gratitude.

Prayer

Dear Jesus,
listen to us.
Call us by name.
Speak tenderly to our hearts.
Take away our fears, so that we, too,
might listen to you, to one another.
Teach us to listen as you listen.
Bring us into that conversation that creates,
that makes us human,
that makes us a community.
You are the Word in our midst,
God's discourse,
God's conversation.
And, wonder of wonders,
you choose us to enter into that conversation
—you want to listen to us,
to listen us into new life.
Open our ears, our lips, and our hearts.

PAUL SOUKUP, S.J., teaches in the Communication Department at Santa Clara University, where he joined the faculty in 1985. He earned his Ph.D. in communication theory, including interpersonal communication, at the University of Texas in Austin, and he also holds a Master of Divinity degree and a Master of Sacred Theology degree from the Jesuit School of Theology at Berkeley. He is particularly interested in the intersection of communication and theology, and he has published multiple books and articles on the subject.

Pauline BOOKS & MEDIA

The Daughters of St. Paul operate book and media centers at the following addresses. Visit, call or write the one nearest you today, or find us on the World Wide Web, www.pauline.org

CALIFORNIA

3908 Sepulveda Blvd, Culver City, CA 90230	310-397-8676
2640 Broadway Street, Redwood City, CA 94063	650-369-4230
5945 Balboa Avenue, San Diego, CA 92111	858-565-9181

FLORIDA

145 S.W. 107th Avenue, Miami, FL 33174	305-559-6715

HAWAII

1143 Bishop Street, Honolulu, HI 96813	808-521-2731
Neighbor Islands call:	866-521-2731

ILLINOIS

172 North Michigan Avenue, Chicago, IL 60601	312-346-4228

LOUISIANA

4403 Veterans Memorial Blvd, Metairie, LA 70006	504-887-7631

MASSACHUSETTS

885 Providence Hwy, Dedham, MA 02026	781-326-5385

MISSOURI

9804 Watson Road, St. Louis, MO 63126	314-965-3512

NEW JERSEY

561 U.S. Route 1, Wick Plaza, Edison, NJ 08817	732-572-1200

NEW YORK

150 East 52nd Street, New York, NY 10022	212-754-1110

PENNSYLVANIA

9171-A Roosevelt Blvd, Philadelphia, PA 19114	215-676-9494

SOUTH CAROLINA

243 King Street, Charleston, SC 29401	843-577-0175

TENNESSEE

4811 Poplar Avenue, Memphis, TN 38117	901-761-2987

TEXAS

114 Main Plaza, San Antonio, TX 78205	210-224-8101

VIRGINIA

1025 King Street, Alexandria, VA 22314	703-549-3806

CANADA

3022 Dufferin Street, Toronto, ON M6B 3T5	416-781-9131

¡También somos su fuente para libros,
videos y música en español!